QUIET

Edited by
Tiddy Rowan

quadrille

The world is becoming progressively noisier, while quietness is being eroded. Our offices, homes and city streets are getting ever louder as we fill our lives with more machinery and electronics. We are bombarded by rising decibels from traffic, machinery, excavation, building works and air traffic. The explosion of mobile phones, computers and gadgets, in the hands of an ever-increasing population is engulfing us. The effects of noise on all of us are pernicious, even though the sources often go unchallenged.

A report on the health effects of noise, published by the World Health Organisation in 2011, found that in Western Europe, excessive noise was second only to air pollution as a cause of environmental ill-health.

The Economist

We are having to go further afield to find quiet – to get away from the noise we make. More remote places to holiday, quiet compartments in trains and headphones to block out noise ...

... but we are also seeking other ways of achieving a quieter life and less troubled minds through mindfulness and other stress-reducing practices.

"A happy life must be to a great extent a quiet life, for it is only in an atmosphere of quiet that true joy can live."

BERTRAND RUSSELL

According to reports, noisy open plan offices are making workers 66% less productive. What we hear drastically affects our stress levels, our productivity and our moods – even for extrovert personality types. For introverts, it is particularly stressful when they need to have solitude to focus on their work, recharge and not have their energies dissipated.

Extrovert behaviour became prevalent in the commercial post-industrial society when everyone found themselves having to sell something – their services, their products, their advertising skills, their art and even their marriagability. Inevitably those that spoke the loudest and the most persuasively got the deal. Extroverts thrived in this atmosphere. People of a naturally quieter disposition – the introverts – struggled to be heard.

"Silence is for me a fount of healing which makes my life worth living. Talking is often a torrent for me, and I need many days of silence to recover from the futility of words."

CARL JUNG

Despite the fact that one third of the general population are introverts, until recently it was one of the most misunderstood personality traits. Although society tends to think highly of extrovert qualities such as assertiveness and outspokenness over solitude and quiet contemplation, there is now a growing appreciation of the values of introverts. And it is not just the growing acceptance of introverts. Extrovert personalities who are experiencing increasing levels of stress are realising the benefit of turning inwards to find their own centre of calm.

The popular opinion is that introverts are shy whilst extroverts are outgoing. But the definition is more complex than that. The stumbling block stems from not having a clear understanding of the distinction between introversion and extroversion.

" There is something greater and purer than what the mouth utters. Silence illuminates our souls, whispers to our hearts, and brings them together."

KAHLIL GIBRAN
The Broken Wing

The famous Swiss psychologist and psychotherapist, Carl Jung, was the first person to postulate the terms introversion and extroversion in his book *Psychological Types* published in 1921, nominating different personalities or personality types as either introvert or extrovert. He stated that extroverts are more naturally oriented towards the outside world, and introverts more focused on their own inner world. He surmised that introverts are drained of energy by too much stimuli and gain energy from solitude and quiet, whereas extroverts are highly sociable and gain energy from being with other people.

The '–vert' ending in extrovert and introvert gives the root meaning to both words because 'vert' in Latin means 'to turn'. Therefore, people are either inclined to turn inwards for energy or to turn outwards for energy and fuel.

These describe the essentially predominant traits in the two personality types, but as in all human behaviour, people fluctuate all the time and even extreme introverts and extroverts do not always act according to their type. There may not be loud in all of us, but there is a core of quiet in everyone, however deep or inaccessible it may seem.

With a little practice, mindfulness can take us to a quiet place.

Switch off your phone and make sure that you're in a place where you won't be interrupted or disturbed.

Find a comfortable position to sit or lie down and start with a few breathing exercises.

Breathe in counting to five, hold for two counts and let your breath out over a count of five.

Then let your breathing find its own natural rhythm whilst you relax your whole body from head to toe.

Now take your mind to a quiet place – somewhere you've visited. Immerse yourself.

When we know where we are on the introversion/extroversion scale, we can be more confident in choosing what degree of social stimuli we need and similarly be confident in being able to withdraw when we've had enough.
No one says we have to be the last to leave the party.

Now that everyone is connected via the internet, more emphasis is being placed on achieving higher emotional intelligence (EQ) to empathise and negotiate positively with others in a global economy. In other words, paying more attention to enhancing our people skills.

To be a good listener is considered a key people skill. An essential requirement of being a good listener is to be quiet when other people are talking.

"Quiet people have the loudest minds."

STEPHEN HAWKING

The percentage ratio commonly arrived at between introverts and extroverts is 30%/70%. Which is why we all need balance and understanding.

According to sound engineers, noise is classified by its audible frequencies and associated with a colour, based on where it falls on the spectrum of high to low frequencies. White noise is different in that it contains sound across all frequencies. It is effective in blocking out audio distractions and so it's a great aid for reading, writing, working and studying. The sound is a gentle hissing noise and can be adjusted to your optimum level.

"At last builders and architects are taking sound seriously... It is becoming as important as other elements of design in the home. We are inundated by consumers wanting peace and quiet."

POPPY ELLIOTT
Managing Director of
www.quietmark.com

Quiet Mark is an awards scheme that seeks out and certifies everything from gadgets, kettles and washing machines to cars, heavy machinery and lawnmowers. It recommends manufacturers who pay close attention to achieving particularly low noise levels.

Break the habit of going straight to your mobile phone to check for messages and emails when you have quiet moments. You don't have to be on call and available 24 hours of the day. Use the time to practise being quiet.

Our intuition is there to guide us. But we can't hear our intuition in a loud and frantic environment. It is important to factor in some quiet time every day in order to stay tuned in.

> *"With an eye made quiet by the power of harmony, and the deep power of joy, we see into the life of things."*

WILLIAM WORDSWORTH
Lines Composed a Few Miles above Tintern Abbey

In Jim Collins's book *Good To Great* he examined the business models of 11 high-achieving companies and found that their leaders, contrary to expectation and despite being very determined, turned out to be quiet, self-effacing and even shy people.

"Wise men speak because they have something to say; fools because they have to say something."

PLATO

" We find so many people impatient to talk... All this talking can hardly be said to be of any benefit to the world. It is so much waste of time."

MAHATMA GANDHI

Group brainstorming sessions and open plan offices tend to suit extroverts but, may have a subduing effect on more introverted colleagues. This leads to less productive work.

Introversion is more common and its defining values more valued in the East than in the West.

"The Wise Man believes profoundly in silence – the sign of a perfect equilibrium. Silence is the absolute poise or balance of body, mind and spirit. The man who preserves his selfhood ever calm and unshaken by the storms of existence – not a leaf, as it were, astir on the tree, not a ripple upon the surface of the shining pool – his, in the mind of the unlettered sage, is the ideal attitude and conduct of life. Silence is the cornerstone of character."

OHIYESA (DR. CHARLES ALEXANDER EASTMAN)
Santee Sioux

With advertising campaigns and media reports becoming increasingly celebrity driven, the public is urged more and more to copy other people's activities. This creates a frantic environment which is the opposite of the calm and quiet we all need in order to flourish and grow independently.

Religious and spiritual leaders, savants and sages including, Moses and Jesus, are often characterised by their need to go off alone and find quiet in order to experience revelations that they later share with their followers.

Many gifted artists and writers, such as J.D. Salinger, Harper Lee, Emily Dickinson and Marcel Proust, all worked best alone. They were often considered recluses when in fact they were merely introverts who found freedom in the quiet and drew inner energy from it.

Inspirational solutions, ground-breaking inventions and great ideas are often results of quiet time spent in solitude.

Despite the constant battle against loud voices trying to drown them out, many notable people in history, such as Mahatma Gandhi, Nelson Mandela and Mother Teresa, have distinguished themselves by being heard despite their quiet voices and personalities.

"Retire into yourself, but first prepare to receive yourself there."

MICHEL DE MONTAIGNE
On Solitude

"*Quiet minds cannot be perplexed or frightened but go on in fortune or misfortune at their own private pace, like a clock during a thunderstorm.*"

ROBERT LOUIS STEVENSON
The Strange Case of Dr. Jekyll and Mr. Hyde

For good reasons, kindergarten schools promote quiet times during the day. When children become over excited and clamorous, a quiet time acts as a pressure valve and gives them a chance to become calm and focused.

It can be challenging parenting an introverted child in an extroverted world. Schools tend to be designed for louder children and mistakenly the parents of introverts try to fix them.

The same could be said of boot-camp team building sessions in the workplace and business groups where it seems only extroversion has a chance at succeeding.

As a mindfully quiet exercise make a list of all the quiet and relaxing music you like e.g. Ludwig van Beethoven's *Moonlight Sonata* or Steve Roach's *Quiet Music*.

Make a point of listening out for more 'quiet' music that you can add to your playlist for future quiet thinking periods.

The same with art, list the pictures that come to mind that are contemplative and restful e.g. Claude Monet's *Water Lilies* or Robert Rauschenberg's *White Painting*.

Make a point when you're next in an art gallery to seek out more 'quiet' art work.

" Silence is so accurate."

MARK ROTHKO

There are surprising areas of quiet and calm that can be found amidst even the most crowded areas.

- Many airports provide quiet areas or relaxation zones and even sleep pods. Download 'Priority Pass', a free app for iPhones and smart phones, and it will locate the nearest quiet lounge to you and give you details and directions.

- Multi-faith chapels in airports and hospitals provide a quiet space where phones, laptops and tannoy systems are not allowed.

Time is our most precious currency.
It is up to us how we manage it.
Spending some of it in quiet
moments is time well spent.

Regardless of your character type, it's good to spend time being mindfully quiet. An exercise to access this is to concentrate on your senses.

- Close your eyes and listen.

- Summon up your favourite smell and imagine you can inhale and savour it.

- Touch whatever your hands are resting on – the fold of a fabric, the cuff of a shirt or the feel of the furniture.

- Open your eyes and take in what you can see and study it carefully – the shapes and the colours. Then return to the world of sound with refreshed ears.

Traditionally, women were expected to be quieter and more passive than men, making it easier for female introverts to stay below the radar. In contemporary society it is a different story, with women being encouraged to be sassy, bold and often more extroverted than their essential personalities (if they are more introvertly inclined).

There has been a pervasive sense that there is something wrong with being an introvert, because that's been the conventional thinking for so long. Part of this thinking has been the lack of understanding about the true meaning of the word. Just as there are different blood groups, there are different personality groups. People need and thrive in different energy sources.

Knowledge and understanding create balance. Working in groups and collaboration will always be vital, but understanding that people need to arrive at these groups having percolated their ideas, in a way that best suits them, is also vital.

After all, throughout mankind's history, we have seen that solitude is essential for the mind and the soul to breathe and for creativity to flourish.

Meditation and mindfulness are terms that seem abstract and inaccessible unless practised. But when you cut through the layers of meaning and activity, in its purest, most simple form, meditation is the activity of non-activity. It's simply adopting a comfortable but preferably straight-backed sitting position and allowing the time to be still and quiet.

"I restore myself when I am alone."

MARILYN MONROE

"*The only thing nicer than a phone that didn't ring all the time (or indeed at all) was six phones that didn't ring all the time (or indeed at all).*"

DOUGLAS ADAMS
The Restaurant at the End of the Universe

Harmony is finding a balance in everything. Creating quiet in our lives is the perfect antidote to the frantic and often noisy side of our existence. For each of us that balance will be different according to how busy, stressful or quiet our lives already are. But finding it is the same journey.

"During intense concentration when the body needs to create 'quiet' it utilises a mechanism whereby blood flow is diverted to brain regions that process relevant, rather than random, sounds, says Jyoti Mishra, an attention researcher at the University of California, San Francisco. That's why we can tune out ticking clocks, passing cars, and even hearing our own name being called when we are intensely focused or preoccupied."

KATHERINE SCHREIBER
Psychology Today

It's important to understand one's own basic nature, when choosing holidays. Introverts need to recharge from within, so their vacations should be chosen accordingly. An extrovert, who is energised by external energy, needs to go to places that will stimulate them. This understanding can be helpful in sorting out family trips or holidays with a friend!

More people need to speak up to quiet down the music volume in restaurants and coffee shops.

Nowadays, there's more on the menu than just food and drink. Loud music on top of the noise of people shouting over it – creates even more noise. It's time to choose our places to meet according to sound factors as well as the menu.

There are times to be loud – in appreciation, encouragement, making music and celebration. But equally there are times to be quiet. It is a question of balance.

" The best cure for the body is a quiet mind."

NAPOLEON BONAPARTE

Retreats are periods of solitude for reflection and recharging. Make it a habit to have a mini retreat every day which is devoted to being quiet.

Introverts at the lower end of the scale – the extremely sensitive ones – are more prone to depression. Mindfulness is helpful in bringing them out of themselves and enabling them to be more comfortable around other people.

Extroverts at the higher end of the scale are prone to stress and stress-related anxieties. Mindfulness is helpful for them to destress, focus and find peace and quiet in their lives.

"After silence, that which comes nearest to expressing the inexpressible is music."

ALDOUS HUXLEY
Music at Night and Other Essays

There would be no music without the spaces – the silence – between the notes.

Some musicians who play regularly benefit from a period of quiet before they perform. Practising mindfulness helps the musician to become centered, to be present, to become free of fears and to reconnect directly with their music. The practice can be alone or a shared moment of quiet.

"Silence is like fertile soil, which, as it were, awaits our creative act, our seed."

ARVO PÄRT

We are individuals and cannot be expected to flourish whilst following imposed herding. If we are allowed to develop ideas and communicate them according to our own individual natures and characters, whether quiet or loud, it will boost creativity and productivity.

The fact that schools, government, healthcare institutions and businesses are endorsing mindfulness practices indicates the growing awareness that there needs to be more balance in society between loud and quiet people.

By introducing mindfulness practices in schools, listening skills in pupils will be improved.

Acknowledging the inner strength
and good listening skills of introverts
is not to denigrate extroverts who
also have many positive attributes,
but instead recognises that the
world needs both types of individual for
the well-being of society and business.

"*I think a lot, but I don't say much.*"

ANNE FRANK
The Diary of a Young Girl

Mindfulness and steady breathing are helpful aides to provide calm, control and power to the voice.

The noisier the world we live in and the environment in which we work and communicate, the harder it is to pay attention to the people and things in life that are quiet, subtler and more understated.

*" The quieter you become,
the more you can hear."*

RAM DASS

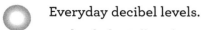

Everyday decibel levels.

10 decibels: Falling leaves.

20 decibels: A whisper in a quiet library.

30 decibels: Quiet conversation.

40 decibels: The noise level in an average house or the hum of a fridge.

50 decibels: Normal office noise or rainfall.

60–70 decibels: Piano practice or the noise of a normal conversation at 3ft apart.

70 decibels: Level at which most people play their radio.

80 decibels: Noisy office or an alarm clock, loud singing or the average sound of traffic.

100 decibels: Bass drum, passing truck or a car horn.

110 decibels: Screaming child.

120 decibels: Rock concert.

180 decibels: Plane taking off.

JEROME BURNE

"*Buy the best headphones you possibly can afford ... Don't be afraid to put your fingers in your ears if you're stuck in a loud environment without adequate protection.*"

JULIAN TREASURE
www.thesoundagency.com

" *We are surrounded by the sounds of the machinery that makes our lives comfortable and convenient. The constant thrum of traffic, the thunder of jet engines overhead. But when we listen to these noises for too long or at the wrong time, they can inflict silent and stealthy damage. Increasing evidence shows this damage isn't just to our ears, but to our blood vessels and heart.* "

JEROME BURNE

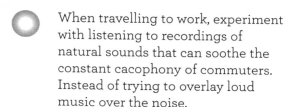

When travelling to work, experiment with listening to recordings of natural sounds that can soothe the constant cacophony of commuters. Instead of trying to overlay loud music over the noise.

Improve your listening skills – mindfully.

Spend five minutes a day closing your eyes and 'listening' to silence.

"I like to listen. I have learned a great deal from listening carefully. Most people never listen."

ERNEST HEMINGWAY

In general, of the 60% of time spent listening, only 25% of what is said is retained.

"The world is but a perpetual see-saw."

MICHEL DE MONTAIGNE

There needs to be a quiet balance. It's not about creating a totally silent world but creating one that respects quiet more, so that somewhere in the middle of the noise continuum (both in sound as well as in personality types) there is a mutually respected meeting point. See-saws work as a simple example of a mechanical system with two equilibrium positions. It is up to everyone to keep their see-saw even!

In an increasingly noisy world, entertainment and culture has had to become increasingly gratuitous and intoxicating to get noticed. Tannoy messages become ever louder to be heard above the hubbub. Historic museums and art galleries now have shops and video simulations of the experience, which all add to the cacophony and confusion. Making a habit of withdrawing from the hurly-burly of the outside world gives us a chance to get past the unscrambling mechanism of our minds to the kernel of stillness that lies within.

If you want peace –
relax completely.

Even if you don't want to commit to a meditation or mindfulness programme, you can still dip in and find exercises or practices that will be helpful in finding moments of peace, relaxation, harmony and quiet. The more you practise the more you will find.

Quiet people (but not necessarily shy people) function better in low key and small group discussions and are often panicked by having to speak in public. One of the reasons for this is that their ability to focus is impaired by heightened stimulation, which disrupts their short-term memory and renders them unable to retrieve information. Extroverts, on the other hand, are generally more spontaneous talkers and thrive in highly social situations. They are energised by being in front of a large group of people and are able to convey their thoughts coherantly.

Introverts cannot always be protected by their shells. Sometimes they must come out of their comfort zone and speak up.

" To sin by silence when they should protest, makes cowards of men. "

ELLA WHEELER WILCOX
An Ambitious Man

People who are naturally quiet or who find it difficult to speak up in group discussions or public speaking may find it helpful to be coached in how to overcome their fears.

Cities are full of excitement, business and buzz. But however much we enjoy city life, everyone needs to reconnect with nature once in a while to feel renewed.

Tips for public speaking.

- Work to control filler words.

- Practice, pause and breathe.

- Greet some of the audience members as they arrive. It's easier to speak to a group of friends than to strangers.

- Know the room. Arrive early, walk around the speaking area and practise using the microphone and any visual aids.

- Relax. Begin by addressing the audience. It buys you time and calms your nerves. Pause, smile and count to three before saying anything. Transform nervous energy into enthusiasm.

- Realize that people want you to succeed. Audiences want you to be interesting, stimulating, informative and entertaining. They're rooting for you.

- Don't apologize for any nervousness or problem – the audience probably never noticed it.

- Concentrate on the message – not the medium. Focus your attention away from your own anxieties and concentrate on your message and your audience.

TOASTMASTERS INTERNATIONAL
www.toastmasters.org

If you cannot leave the city, then make time every day to find a green space, however small, in which to contemplate quietly for ten minutes. Or weather permitting, take your lunch to a green space for an hour instead of eating at your desk or joining the throng of public eating places.

Check out the art galleries or churches close to where you live and where you work. Take time out of a busy day and spend five to ten minutes studying a piece of art or architecture that attracts you.

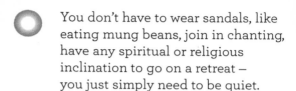

You don't have to wear sandals, like
eating mung beans, join in chanting,
have any spiritual or religious
inclination to go on a retreat —
you just simply need to be quiet.

Think of a retreat as a mind-holiday – you will return having cleared your mind, experienced stillness and quiet and found that same peace within. Eventually able to hear yourself again in the frenzied everyday world.

Close your eyes, take a normal, natural breath, let it out slowly and be aware of that quiet within. Do this whenever you need to change the tempo, bring yourself back to the realisation of the present moment, or before reflecting on what you need to do or say next.

You don't even have to close your eyes. You can do this anywhere – without having to leave the room or the conversation. Your breath is the key – letting it power you back to the present moment and whatever you need to focus on.

" Whether people first hear about the two kinds of perception and two kinds of judgment as children, high school students, parents or grandparents, the richer development of their own type can be a rewarding adventure for the rest of their lives."

ISABEL BRIGGS MYERS

The Myers-Briggs personality test assesses peoples' personality types and the results are used to help employers and employees find their most suitable role within the workplace.

Emotional intelligence (EQ) is the ability to identify and manage our own emotions and to identify the emotional state and needs of other people and how to respond to them as appropriately and efficiently as situations and circumstances demand. This understanding and sensitivity comes more easily to some people (those noted to have EQ) than others. To arrive at these indentifications of emotional content in ourselves and in others requires time spent in quiet contemplation.

" Most people assume that meditation is all about stopping thoughts, getting rid of emotions, somehow controlling the mind. But actually it's ... about stepping back, seeing the thought clearly, witnessing it coming and going."

ANDY PUDDICOMBE
Co-founder of Headspace
www.getsomeheadspace.com

Libraries offer oases of calm on busy days to relax, read or work quietly. Not only should we fight to keep libraries going, but we should speak up to have areas of them kept quiet.

The more we can attune to other people's individual needs and personality traits with compassion, the more we will be aware of the noise or disturbance we may be creating around them.

To create balance...

An extrovert needs to accept his or her introverted partner's need for space, while an introvert needs to acknowledge his or her extroverted partner's need for social interaction.

"I hold this to be the highest task for a bond between two people: that each protects the solitude of the other."

RAINER MARIA RILKE
Letters to a Young Poet

Working on the internet, screened from the world yet connected to it, is a good place for introverts to exert their knowledge and business leadership. They don't have to think on their feet – instead they can organise a quiet time to think through their strategies before exposing them.

Extrovert colleagues are best at using their skills for public speaking or sales pitches, whilst introverts excel at focusing and preparing presentations. If each type recognises and understands each other's strengths, they can work together instead of clashing or trying to master each other's areas of expertise.

With this understanding, quiet and loud colleagues can go further in their careers and learn more skills from each other.

With this open-minded exchange, the barriers between the two personality types can be lowered and a positive synergy can arise.

The other plus in learning to understand your personality type is discovering the ability to shift between your different attributes. Knowing when to hold back, when to exercise a more assertive stance; when to speak up and when to keep quiet.

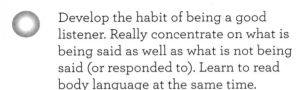

Develop the habit of being a good listener. Really concentrate on what is being said as well as what is not being said (or responded to). Learn to read body language at the same time.

Good Listening Tips.

- Make time for one-to-one telephone calls – not whilst doing something else.

- Make a habit of bringing yourself back to the present moment when you feel your mind wandering to other things. With practice you will be able to find a prompt that helps you to come back to what is being said.

- When having a conversation, by telephone or face to face, commit to focusing on it as a requirement.

- If a friend or colleague needs to express their feelings or give voice to their anger, sorrow or dilemma, then you need to give them time. They are talking to you for a reason and entrusting you to help them.

- By periodically reflecting back to the speaker what you understand the conversation to be about, you are letting the other person know that you are engaged and you are also putting into context your understanding of the conversation.

The Power of the Pause.

A gap in the conversation doesn't have to be filled. Often it makes a stronger point to either stop talking or to not answer a question straightaway. People are afraid of breaks in conversation and tend to fill them for the sake of avoiding silence – without too much thought of the content. Leaving a gap open can be a way of drawing people out.

Speaking up.

- Before beginning a presentation or speaking in public ensure you arrive early.

- Take five minutes of quiet to yourself. Stand or sit in a confident pose, drop your shoulders and breathe in to the count of five. Hold your breath for two and let it out slowly on the count of about five.

- Keep focusing on your breathing until it settles to a natural and comfortable level.

The centre, or eye, of a typhoon is quiet, still and calm, playing an intrinsic part in how these weather systems take shape.

This is the same with the deeper mind, or subconscious – right in the centre is extreme quiet despite any turbulence on the surface. Practising meditation or mindfulness is one way of accessing that quiet centre.

On a commuter train – always choose the quiet carriage, when possible.

You will arrive at work recharged instead of frazzled by erratic phone calls, having to listen to the conversations of others and the constant noise of text alerts and 'leaking' headphones. Instead use the time to think, switch off or quietly read or work with noise-blocking headphones.

In your work environment resolve to have lunch for an hour by yourself – at least once a week – somewhere quiet. Having lunch at your desk surrounded by noise and people doesn't give your system a much-needed chance to recharge during the day.

> *"All men's miseries derive from not being able to sit in a quiet room alone."*

BLAISE PASCAL

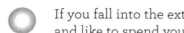

If you fall into the extrovert category and like to spend your working day interacting with colleagues in meetings, discussions, lunch dates and drinks after work, you would still reap the benefits from factoring in some daily quiet time in order to allow your inner creativity to come to the surface. Subconscious thinking needs space to germinate. Practising mindfulness and focusing on your breathing really helps create an atmosphere of calm. It allows the mind to settle and the subconscious to find solutions, in a way that is impossible when under a constant bombardment of data, people and noise.

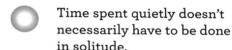

Time spent quietly doesn't necessarily have to be done in solitude.

There is a supportive and comforting energy in being around other people who also need to be quiet. Being in a library or café means you can work or study on your laptop with earphones to create a ring of quiet around you. You can also use your laptop as a 'prop' – to access your music or natural sound recordings, or plug in noise-blocking headphones so that you actually can spend time in quiet thought.

In a society that endorses multi-screens at home, iPhones and iPads, families are increasingly split into factions. Reading, colouring-in, board games, playing cards or cooking together are still key activities; their prime importance is that they connect us to others, inducing a sense of fun and a quiet solidarity for children and adults alike.

For people who say it is impossible to find any time to spend quietly, the answer is to get up half an hour earlier.

It's the quietest time of the day – less traffic noise outside, less email pings and phone rings to interrupt us. Although at first it seems a sacrifice to your precious sleep – after three days the habit starts to form and the benefits make any sacrifice seem worthwhile. Decide on a positive strategy for that half an hour. No emails, calls or making lists. Walking, jogging, yoga, singing, practising mindfulness or even gardening are all great ways to start the day.

Jeff Weiner (LinkedIn CEO) puts quiet slots in his schedule every day that are free of meetings so that he has time to reflect and think strategically.

"My imagination functions much better when I don't have to speak to people."

PATRICIA HIGHSMITH

'Peace and quiet' is a phrase that is commonly used but rarely understood. At the centre of quiet there is a refuge, a safe place free from discussion, explanation and judgement. This is an oasis where we can refresh our minds, spirits and bodies and find our quiet haven – our peace.

For people on the quieter end of the scale it is important to recognise that too much time spent in solitude can also weigh the see-saw down. Ideas and creativity may be constantly bubbling away, but now and again we need to get out there and share them, to engage in face to face business and social meetings and get-togethers.

"Be silent or let thy words be worth more than silence."

PYTHAGORAS

When we find ourselves with time on our hands, it's usually quiet time – waiting for someone to turn up to a meeting or a get-together, a doctor's appointment or waiting for a train. Instead of being agitated by the lost time, see it as valuable moment that can be spent practising a simple mindfulness exercise.

- Close your eyes or tilt your head down about 45 degrees and focus on a spot near you.

- Don't change anything, just watch the gentle rise and fall of your breath.

- When your mind wanders, gently bring your attention back to your breathing and you will soon find a sense of calm.

Spending quality quiet time brings our minds back to the present moment instead of constantly anticipating what will happen next in life.

Knowing when to keep quiet is an important learning curve.

"Better to remain silent and be thought a fool than to speak out and remove all doubt."

ABRAHAM LINCOLN

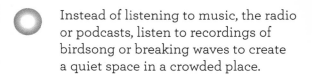

Instead of listening to music, the radio
or podcasts, listen to recordings of
birdsong or breaking waves to create
a quiet space in a crowded place.

If introverts as a group are more sensitive than extroverts, then it is easy to see why they are drawn inherently towards jobs or vocations where sensitivity plays a role: nurses, doctors, scholars, negotiators, philosophers, artists and musicians. Extroverts, who generally have thicker skins, are temperamentally better suited to being politicians, presenters, project managers and sales people. So understanding our introvert/ extrovert type is conducive to selecting a job or a career best suited to our personal sensibilities.

The same may be true of finding a partner. An extremely introverted person and an extremely extroverted individual may struggle to enjoy the same things – the extrovert needs a busy social life, parties and cramming a lot into a day off or holiday time, while the introvert prefers taking things slower and not going out every night. But again, it's a question of balance. We should stop trying to mould our partners into an extension of ourselves or into people we would prefer them to be. Take them as they are and work around it.

The vocal chords need exercise in order to give your voice presence and command attention from an audience.

- Practise daily basic singing exercises (especially in the shower).

- Speak tongue twisters out loud in front of the mirror.

- Record your voice so that you can adjust your tone or pitch and evaluate the clarity of your speech.

"*Would you like to be one of those people for whom others instinctively fall quiet and really listen? An important aspect of quiet is what you want from people when you are talking. In other words you want to learn how to speak so people listen.*"

JULIAN TREASURE
www.thesoundagency.com

"Powerful speaking (not just public speaking) is an invaluable skillset. The human voice is the most powerful sound on this planet; it can make us laugh, cry, feel inspired and even change the world. Whether you're teaching your child, chasing a prospective client, asking for a raise from your boss or even proposing marriage to your partner, what you say and the way you say it will determine the outcome. Making ourselves heard is a challenge simply because most of us have never been trained to speak effectively."

JULIAN TREASURE
www.thesoundagency.com

For most of us, being heard doesn't happen naturally. A key skill in influencing and impacting on others is down to powerful speaking.

Think about:

- How you breathe.
- Your body language.
- Your intonation.
- The confidence you exude.
- Your command of language.

"Listening is our access to understanding... Just three minutes a day of silence is a wonderful exercise to reset your ears and to recalibrate so that you can hear the quiet again. If you can't get absolute silence, go for quiet, that's absolutely fine."

JULIAN TREASURE
www.thesoundagency.com

Turn down the noise
and hear yourself think.

Decreasing our stress levels
increases our calm levels.

Take a few moments to stop and notice whatever sounds are going on around you at the moment.

- It could be a car horn, people chatting, the hum of a computer, the refrigerator or the wind in the trees.

- Focus your awareness on these sounds and really listen to them.

- Don't attach any thought to the sounds. Just listen and observe them.

If tensions and voices are rising and an argument or confrontation is imminent, the age-old adage of counting to ten is still valid. It also gives us a chance to find a space in our head to rationalise and react mindfully instead of explosively or mindlessly.

It's good to take stock and start to become aware of other people's perceptions and reception of the noises we create. We aren't always aware of the noise we make in our daily activities: banging doors, talking loudly on the phone in someone else's space or even shouting conversations from another room.

Arthur Schopenhauer was a German philosopher (1788–1860) who complained of how constant, intrusive noise plagued his life. The impact of this constant disturbance led him to assert that noise and the lack of a quiet environment was not conducive to critical thinking or creativity.

"A man can be himself only so long as he is alone, and if he does not love solitude, he will not love freedom, for it is only when he is alone that he is really free."

ARTHUR SCHOPENHAUER

Before the value of property rose
and the average size of living space
dwindled, there used to be more room
for everyone to carve out their own
personal space.

"*A woman must have money and a room of her own if she is to write...*"

VIRGINIA WOOLF
A Room of One's Own

In a relationship – especially a live-in one where physical space is limited – we all need our own 'head space' from time to time. If we don't find it, we're apt to react negatively in some way. Our quiet time and their quiet time don't always coincide. By being aware, being mindful of the other person's needs, expressions and behaviour, we can subtly give them the space they need – both in time and place.

Where space is at a premium, bedrooms are rarely the quiet sanctuaries we would like them to be. They double up as study rooms, dressing rooms, they house gym equipment, storage and beds. Keeping the bed and surrounding area clear allows a refuge from a busy day. Try a week without taking any screens (TV, mobile, iPad or laptop) to bed with you and visualise leaving any work or worrying issues outside the bedroom door. The quality of your sleep will be enhanced.

A community of monks lives at Tassajara Zen Mountain Monastery in California.

"Here was a group of people who'd unplugged from the world of cell phones and 24-hour news presumably to live more contemplative, kinder and less chaotic lives than the rest of us."

COLLEEN MORTON BUSCH
Author, *Fire Monks*

The resources for resolving our problems and making decisions lie within us. But we have to make a quiet space in the mind in order to be able to tune into them. As we watch athletes reaching into the depths of their inner resources to bring out their best – so too can we access our own inner depths to find the strength we need. Making time to access that quiet space is simply a matter of deciding to.

Many of the world's most acclaimed athletes practise quiet mindfulness and meditation before competing. It has been shown to reduce their stress levels, improve their focus and ease their anxiety before high-pressure games, matches or races.

Resting and recharging our mental muscles is just as important as resting and recharging the muscles in our bodies. We can recharge through simple breathing exercises to refresh our busy minds. We should take the opportunity whenever we can to recharge. We tend to live regimented lives when the demands on us are high. Although it is good to have routines, it is also good to give ourselves permission to stop when the need for a quiet place or moment presents itself.

Since introverts are more commonly misunderstood than extroverts, it is helpful to dispel commonly misunderstood stereotypical traits.

- Not all introverts are shy.

- Introverts do enjoy socialising – just not all the time.

- Introverts can make equally good (if not better) leaders than extroverts.

- Although the personalities of introverts are quieter than those of extroverts, this does not mean that they are inherently more negative.

Solitude is different from isolation.
Isolation is cutting yourself off from
others, while solitude is making
friends with yourself so that you can
foster better relationship with others.

The tendency to accumulate 'things' in the house is arrested by either discipline or running out of space. The same can be said of the mind – it is a hoarder's haven of accumulated thoughts from the past and endless must-do lists for the present and the future. Comparing our minds with our physical spaces can help to avoid mental hoarding, it is an incentive to clear our minds of unwanted, out of date, duplicated and chipped thoughts.

Signs that you need some quiet time to mind-clear are irritability, losing your sense of humour, not being able to concentrate or focus on what you are doing and general fatigue. Being aware of these signals means you can use these as prompts to find some space and calm in order to get you back to the present.

"Let's turn down the noise and turn up peace and quiet... The level of noise that we live with really closes us down. People have very little peace and quiet. Silence is not just no noise – silence is peace and quiet. And peace and quiet is therapeutic and very beautiful."

BRUCE DAVIS Ph.D.
www.silentstay.com

"How intense can be the longing to escape from the emptiness and dullness of human verbosity, to take refuge in nature, apparently so inarticulate..."

BORIS PASTERNAK
Doctor Zhivago

" That man's silence is wonderful to listen to."

THOMAS HARDY
Under the Greenwood Tree

Finding quiet times and quiet places to allow our own creativity and character to develop requires patience and practice so that it becomes a habit.

"You do not need to leave your room. Remain sitting at your table and listen. Do not even listen, simply wait, be quiet, still and solitary. The world will freely offer itself to you to be unmasked."

FRANZ KAFKA

If you find working in an open plan office at times stifling to your creative flow or focus – explore quieter and more private parts of the office that might be available from time to time. See if you can book an hour in the meeting room for yourself.

Playing music in public places is partly intended to act as a muffler so that people's conversations can't be heard, but sometimes we can't even hear each other, or ourselves, over it. It is acceptable to ask for the music to be turned down if it is too intrusive. Even if your request is denied, you will have made a valuable point and you can then either stay or find somewhere quieter.

*" The way we're working isn't working ...
In a world of increasing demand
and diminishing resources, people
are working more hours, spending more
time outside work tethered to digital
devices, and taking less time to reflect,
renew and prioritize. As a result, they're
increasingly exhausted, overwhelmed,
and disengaged. It's not a sustainable
way of working for individuals or
for organizations. "*

TONY SCHWARTZ
President & CEO, The Energy Project
www.theenergyproject.com

There is no sound in space.

"Human beings are not computers. We're not meant to run at high speeds, continuously, for long periods of time. Science tells us we're at our best when we move rhythmically between spending and renewing energy – a reality that companies must embrace to fuel sustainable engagement and high performance."

TONY SCHWARTZ
President & CEO, The Energy Project
www.theenergyproject.com

Gordon Hempton is an acoustic ecologist who had a profound experience at the age of 27 experiencing a thunderstorm and realising that he had never really 'listened' before. He says that quiet places are rapidly vanishing – being eroded by human noise pollution – and that silent spaces found in natural settings undisturbed by human activity and sound is completely underrated yet it contributes profoundly to our well-being.
His quest is to protect these places.

There is no World Heritage Acoustic Sanctuary. Should this be a call to arms by purposeful quiet people globally to create and protect such places?

Through practising mindfulness and being quiet, we can listen to our inner voices and distinguish the difference between an instinctive need for food and cravings. Supplying our bodies' needs is vital for good health in knowing which food we need to eat and when not to eat if our systems are overloaded. We don't need diets – we simply need to listen.

" The great decisions of human life have as a rule far more to do with the instincts and other mysterious unconscious factors than with conscious will and well-meaning reasonableness."

CARL JUNG
Modern Man in Search of a Soul

Ultimately, it's about finding that kernel of quiet within and deciding how we want to live our lives. What is presented here has been an attempt at understanding how noise affects that quiet within us and some tips on how to achieve it.

- How to be better heard in a noisy world.

- How making space for quiet in our noisy lives can lead to a better work – life balance in finding the levels of peace and calm that we want and need in our lives, our homes and our work, but most of all within ourselves.

- Some light has been thrown on the distinction between loud people and quiet people, the different personality traits of introversion and extroversion and that in understanding the difference we can forge improved relationships.

- Best of all, in how to improve the relationship we have with ourselves.

BIBLIOGRAPHY

Books mentioned in *The Little Book of Quiet*

Adams, Douglas, *The Restaurant at the End of the Universe* (Pan, 2009)

Collins, Jim, *Good to Great* (Random House Business, 2001)

Frank, Anne, *The Diary of a Young Girl* (Puffin, 2007)

Gibran, Kahlil, *The Broken Wings* (Citadel, 2003)

Hardy, Thomas, *Under the Greenwood Tree* (Wordsworth Editions, 1994)

Huxley, Aldous, *Music at Night and Other Essays* (Harper Collins, 1994)

Jung, Carl, *Modern Man in Search of a Soul* (Routledge, 2001)

Jung, Carl, *Psychological Types* (Princeton University Press, 1976)

de Montaigne, Michel, *On Solitude: The Greatest Thing in the World is to Know How to Live in Yourself* (Penguin, 2009)

Morton Busch, Colleen, *Fire Monks: Zen Mind Meets Wildfire* (Penguin, 2012)

Pasternak, Boris, *Doctor Zhivago* (Vintage Classics, 2002)

Rilke, Rainer Maria, *Letters to a Young Poet* (Penguin Classics, 2012)

Stevenson, Robert Louis, *The Strange Case of Dr. Jeykll and Mr. Hyde* (William Collins, 2010)

Wilcox, Ella Wheeler, *An Ambitious Man* (E.A. Weeks, 1896)

Woolf, Virginia, *A Room of One's Own* (Penguin Classics, 2002)

Wordsworth, William, *Lines Composed a Few Miles above Tintern Abbey* (Cambridge University Press, 1985)

Further Reading

Cain, Susan, *Quiet: The Power of Introverts in a World That Can't Stop Talking* (Penguin, 2013)

Davis, Bruce, *Simple Peace: The Spiritual Life of St. Francis of Assisi* (Authors Choice Press, 2000)

Hempton, Gordon & Grossman, John, *One Square Inch of Silence* (Atria Books, 2010)

Quiet App www.getsomeheadspace.com

Quiet Video *Julian Treasure TED Talks:* www.ted.com/speakers/julian_treasure

Quiet Music Gordon Hempton (available on iTunes)

Websites

www.quietmark.com

www.livinglifefully.com

www.simplynoise.com

www.thesoundagency.com

www.psychologytoday.com

www.juliantreasure.com

www.myersbriggs.org

www.ted.com/speakers/julian_treasure

www.onesquareinch.org

www.getsomeheadspace.com

www.quietplanet.com

www.soundtracker.com

www.healthinsightuk.org

www.toastmasters.org

www.theenergyproject.com

QUOTES ARE TAKEN FROM:

Abraham Lincoln was the 16th president of the United States. He preserved the Union during the U.S. Civil War and brought about the emancipation of slaves.

Aldous Huxley was a British writer and visionary thinker best known for his novel *Brave New World* published in 1932.

Andy Puddicombe is the Co-Founder of Headspace, a meditation app that makes practising daily mindfulness techniques easy.

Anne Frank wrote a diary about her experiences as a Dutch jew hiding from the Germans during World War Two. She gained international fame after her death when her diary was published in 1947.

Arthur Schopenhauer was a German philosopher best known for his book *The World as Will and Idea* published 1818.

Arvo Pärt is an Estonian composer of classical music and the creator tintinnabuli compositions, a new and original musical language.

Bertrand Russell was a British philosopher, mathematician, historian and political activist and a champion of anti-imperialism.

Blaise Pascal was a very influential French mathematician and philosopher, who laid the foundations for the theory of probability.

Boris Pasternak was a Russian poet and novelist. He wrote *Doctor Zhivago* and won the Nobel Prize for Literature in 1958.

Bruce Davis, Ph.D is a spiritual psychologist and teacher of world religions. He is also an author and his works include *The Heart of Healing, The Magical Child Within You* and *The Love Letters of Assisi meet Pope Francis*.

Carl Jung was a revolutionary psychiatrist and psychotherapist. He is best known for having founded analytical psychology.

Colleen Morton Busch writes non-fiction, poetry and fiction and in 2010 wrote the acclaimed *Fire Monks: Zen Mind Meets Wild Fire*.

Douglas Adams was a British writer and dramatist, best known for his *The Hitchhiker's Guide to the Galaxy* series.

Ella Wheeler Wilcox was an American author and poet best known for her work *Poems of Passion*.

Ernest Hemingway was an American writer who won the Pulitzer Prize in 1952 for *The Old Man and the Sea* and received the Nobel Prize for literature in 1954.

Franz Kafka was a German writer who strongly influenced by the existentialist movement. His works include *The Metamorphosis* and *The Castle*.

Gordon Hempton is the Sound Tracker®, an acoustic ecologist. He has produced over 60 albums and is an Emmy awarding-winning sound recordist.

Isabel Briggs Myers was an American writer and co-creator of a personality test known as Myers-Briggs Type Indicator.

Jerome Burne is an award-winning health journalist who contributes regularly to a variety of national newspapers.

Julian Treasure is a top-rated international speaker and author. Collectively his four TED talks, on various aspects of sound and communication, have been viewed seven million times.

Kahlil Gibran was a Lebanese writer, poet and artist and is renowned for his 1923 book *The Prophet*.

Katherine Schreiber is a human health and behaviour writer and editor, who lives in New York.

Mahatma Gandhi was the leader of the Indian nationalist movement against British rule in India. His method of using only non-violent protest to achieve political and social progress has been hugely influential and he inspired later movements to use the same means.

Marilyn Monroe was an iconic American actress, model and singer during the 1950s and early 1960s.

Mark Rothko was a famous American post-war artist recognised for his abstract expressionist work.

Michel de Montaigne was a significant writer and thinker during the French Renaissance.

Napoleon Bonaparte was a great French military commander who rose to prominence during the French Revolution. As Emperor of France he led the country against a series of coalitions in the Napoleonic Wars.

Ohiyesa (Dr. Charles Alexander Eastman) was a Native American writer, reformer and physician. He is considered the first Native American author to write American history from the Native point of view.

Patricia Highsmith was an American novelist well-known for her psychological thrillers, notably *The Talented Mr. Ripley*.

Plato was one of the most important Greek philosophers. He founded the Academy in Athens and was a student of Socrates and taught Aristotle.

Poppy Elliot is the Managing Director of Quiet Mark, a not-for-profit trading arm of the Noise Abatement Society charity, that was launched in 2012.

Pythagoras was a Greek philosopher and mathematician, who the term 'Pythagoras's Theorem' is named after.

Rainer Maria Rilke was an Austrian poet and philosopher, a profound thinker whose poetry has become hugely popular.

Ram Dass is a well-known and highly regarded American spiritual teacher and author of the best-selling book *Be Here Now*.

Robert Louis Stevenson was a Scottish novelist well known for his works *Treasure Island, Kidnapped* and *The Strange Case of Dr. Jekyll and Mr. Hyde*.

Stephen Hawking is the Director of Research at the Centre for Theoretical Cosmology at Cambridge. He was awarded the CBE in 1982 and is a member of the US National Academy of Science.

Thomas Hardy was a poet and novelist. He gained fame for his novels including *Tess of the d'Urbervilles, Far from the Madding Crowd* and *The Mayor of Casterbridge*.

Tony Schwartz is the President and CEO of The Energy Project, a company that presents a better way of working, helping people become more energised, engaged, focused and productive.

Virginia Woolf was a member of the Bloomsbury group and the famous author of *Mrs Dalloway* and *A Room of One's Own*.

William Wordsworth was a major poet and leading light in the Romantic Age in English literature in the 18th and 19th centuries.

PAGE REFERENCES

Page 3: © The Economist Newspaper Limited, London (Sept 2013)

Page 12: Gibran, Kahlil, *The Broken Wings* (Citadel, 2003)

Page 6: copyright of The Bertrand Russell Peace Foundation Ltd. & Taylor & Francis Publishers.

Page 23: www.quietmark.com

Page 27: Wordsworth, William, *Lines Composed a Few Miles Above Tintern Abbey* (Cambridge University Press, 1985)

Page 24: www.quietmark.com

Page 39: de Montaigne, Michel, *On Solitude: The Greatest Thing in the World is to Know How to Live in Yourself* (Penguin, 2009)

Page 40: Stevenson, Robert Louis, *The Strange Case of Dr. Jekyll and Mr. Hyde* (William Collins, 2010)

Page 56: Adams, Douglas, *The Restaurant at the End of the Universe* (Pan, 2009)

Page 58: Schreiber, Katherine, *Carnal Clues: The Physiology of Flow*, Psychology Today (2012)

Page 66: *Music at Night and Other Essays* reprinted by permission of HarperCollins Publishers Ltd © 1931 Huxley, Aldous

Page 69: Pärt, Arvo

Page 74: © Anne Frank Fonds, Basel, www.annefrank.ch

Page 78-79: jeromeburne.com

Page 80: www.thesoundagency.com

Page 81: jeromeburne.com

Page 93: Wilcox, Ella Wheeler, *An Ambitious Man* (E.A. Weeks, 1896)

Page 107: www.getsomeheadspace.com

Page 111: Rilke, Rainer Maria, *Letters to a Young Poet* (Penguin Classics, 2012)

Page 139: de Montaigne, Michel, *On Solitude: The Greatest Thing in the World is to Know How to Live in Yourself* (Penguin, 2009)

Page 144: www.juliantreasure.com/training/master-of-sound-workshops

Page 145: www.juliantreasure.com/training/master-of-sound-workshops

Page 148: www.juliantreasure.com/training/master-of-sound-workshops

Page 157: Woolf, Virginia, *A Room of One's Own* (Penguin Classics, 2002)

Page 160: Used by permission of the author, Colleen Morton Busch, www.colleenmortonbusch.com from her article in www.huffingtonpost.com/colleen-morton-busch/benefits-of-meditation_b_969788.html.

Page 168: www.silentstay.com

Page 169: Pasternak, Boris, *Doctor Zhivago* (Vintage Classics, 2002)

Page 170: Hardy, Thomas, *Under the Greenwood Tree* (Wordsworth Editions, 1994)

Page 175: theenergyproject.com

Page 177: theenergyproject.com

Page 181: Jung, Carl, *Modern Man in Search of a Soul* (Routledge, 2001)

Editorial director Anne Furniss
Creative director Helen Lewis
Editor Romilly Morgan
Editorial assistant Harriet Butt
Designer Emily Lapworth
Production director Vincent Smith
Production controller Emily Noto

First published in 2014 by Quadrille,
an imprint of Hardie Grant Publishing

Quadrille
52-54 Southwark Street
London SE1 1UN
quadrille.com

Reprinted in 2014, 2015, 2017 (twice), 2018
10 9 8 7 6

British Library Cataloguing-in-Publication Data
A catalogue record for this book is available from the British Library.

ISBN: 978 1 84949 516 5

Printed in China